PHOTOZOO

It's true, it's true,
just a chromosome or two---
you look like him,
he looks like you.

Photographs by Roger C. Birkel

Poems by Philip Macht

Roger C. Birkel :
    For Olivia Simone

Philip Macht:
    For David, Isabel, Tony,
        Emily, Sofia, Madeleine,
            Sarah, Eloise, and Danny

Text Copyright© 1999 by Philip Macht
Photographs Copyright© 1999 by Roger C. Birkel
All rights reserved
Library of Congress Card Catalog Number:
#99-073205

ISBN: 0-9672559-0-2

Published in the United States by
The Maryland Zoological Society
Druid Hill Park   Baltimore, MD 21217

Printed in Canada   First Edition

The snow leopard,
a solitary cat,
seldom seen by man,
haunts the Himalayas
from the Punjab to Bhutan.

Like the look of
Rhino Rose?
Like those two
horns
on her nose?
Bet she looks so
oh-so fine-oh
to the other
two-horned rhinos.

Koala, a marsupial like the kangaroos,
lives on eucalyptus leaves
   and chews and chews and chews.
No, koala's not a bear,
   and it can't live just anywhere.
They are even hard to raise in zoos.

Prairie dogs live in a prairie dog town ---
a complex of tunnels underground.
There they sleep, and there they nest,
and there they hang around.

When little prairie dogs grow up
they do not have to roam.
Their parents burrow out of town,
and leave the pups the home.

The walrus floats on icy flows
  upon the icy seas.
Wrapped in six inch blubber....
  that's why they don't freeze.

A master of disguise,
the tawny frogmouth waits to ambush prey
that doesn't have a hunch
the bird is not a branch
until too late. Surprise!
The prey is lunch.

The Komodo dragon
is an awesome beast
ten feet long and three feet tall.
        It doesn't take a wizard
        to figure out this lizard
is the mother of them all.

A mighty croc
on a smart
stake-out
is a fisher
with a plan.
But the gavial
with its
slender snout
is not a
threat to man.

The gorilla huffs and puffs
and hoots and roars
and howls and bluffs
and rants and taunts---
and then sits anywhere he wants.

In the old days
in Tibet
red panda was a
household pet.

Our national emblem
had fatal problems
the world just didn't
foresee.
What did the birds in...
were egg shells too thin,
a function of DDT.

And for a while there
we heard from
 the scholars
we'd only see eagles
when looking at dollars.

But since we banned it,
we now have discovered
we're feeling better,
and the eagle
 recovered.

The buffalo is coming back,
 (There are ranches in Dakota)
because their steaks are low in fat.
 (A joke to the Lakota).

Sometimes life is funny,
 you have to laugh at how it goes.
The Sioux now run casinos,
 and the whites run buffalos.

Aardvarks make
    disgusting pets.
They mess your shoes
    and claw your pants,
scratch your uncles
    and eat your ants.

Orangutan, orangutan.
Orangutan
is close to man.
Swap a couple genes around---
you're in the trees,
he's on the ground.

The crowned crane,
    a great beauty,
        doing its duty,
            announces events of the day.
And all of its peers
    are always all ears
        to hear what the crane has to say.

Jackals can hunt and they have to,
hunt with a great deal of skill.
They can't count on a meal
from what they can steal
raiding the lion pride's kill.

The babirusa, a wild Asian pig,
has tusks that grow from underneath
that cut right through the snout.
As useless as our wisdom teeth,
but who's to pull them out?

The pygmy chimp, the bonobo,
   is thought by people in the know
      to be our most related.
They're fun to watch, but what you see
   is bound to lead you to agree
      they are the most X-rated.

Sea lions are performers
who like to put on shows.
And best of all, to balance a ball
on a very clever nose.

The tiger studies the crowd.
In his mind's eye
are we deer
grazing by?

The discus fish
make quite a show.
Beauties of the Amazon
and the Orinoco.

<u>Hippopotamus</u>
The hippo's name means river horse,
but no one tries to ride one.
The story is: a Greek who did
ended up inside one.

An elephant's trunk is more than a nose.
It's a versatile tool and a high-pressure hose,
and a trumpet that only an elephant blows.

They say the little rock hyrax,
which looks somewhat like a rat,
is close cousin to the elephant.
Hard to picture that.

The hunter is the lioness,
the lion guards territory.
The lioness does the heavy work,
the lion gets the glory.
He also gets the lioness,
but that's another story.

They say that Mrs. Proboscis
is attracted to Mr. P's big nose.
She stares at him, he pouts at her,
and so it goes, and so it goes.

Some farmers tame the banteng,
though very few know how
to change this Asian bovine
into a Bali cow.

Doesn't love berries.
Doesn't love nuts.
The marabou stork
has the culture
of the vulture.
It goes for guts.

A crocodile with a three foot smile
is not a friendly face.
He glides around the river Nile
like he thinks he owns the place.

Jaguars are great fishers.
They do it with their paws.
They flip a fish to the riverbank,
or catch it in their jaws.

The zebra is a
stunning sight
of white on black...
(or black on white).

Polar bears are great swimmers
when in the wild and free.
Sailors say they've seen them
fifty miles out on the open sea.

The secret of the camel
    is buried in the humps
        where precious fat is stored
           in one (or two) big lumps.

A car can get to sixty in six.
Think that's fast?
Well, a cheetah just ran past.
    They accelerate
     so remarkably
     they can get up to
     sixty in three!

The peacock makes a splendid show
    to catch the peahen's eye.
" See me, I'm irresistible ......
    don't try to pass me by."
The peahen finds him stunning.
That fan really makes it.
And the best is yet to come----
    the "eyes" dance when he shakes it.

The python's a constrictor,
a mighty afflicter,
who can do pretty much
as it pleases.
For who can talk back
when caught in its wrap
as it squeezes
and squeezes
and squeezes.

The cape buffalo, a formidable foe,
   can toss a big cat in the air.
From the caution they show it,
   the lions must know it.......
      and choose something else for their fare.

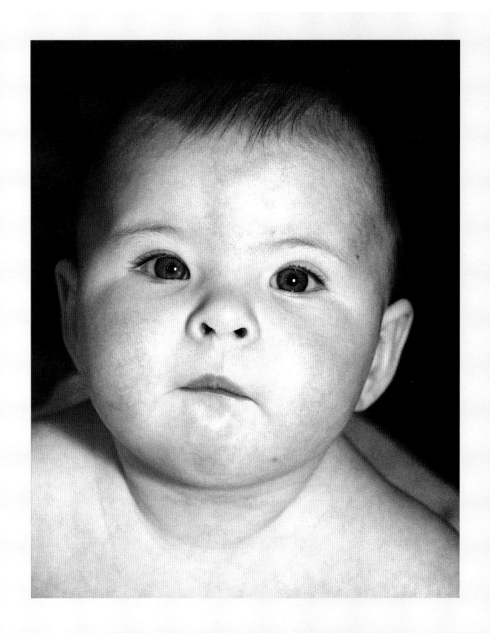

Humans have so much to know
and such a long, long way to go.

A kangaroo baby is called a joey.
Joey lives in mom's pouch for a year.
Oh, he comes out to play and explore,
but dives back, head first, when in fear.

At times
there is nothing
one can say.
The beauty
of the image
takes your
breath away.

The pelican
with its mighty wings
skims just
above the sea.
    Then in a flash,
     a dive, a splash...
into the fishery.

They stand tall.
And with sharp eyes
giraffes can save
the other animals
from harm
by sending out
the quick alarm
that robs the lions
of their prize.

The lemur is our cousin;
very distant cousin, yes,
who got stuck in Madagascar
and never did progress.

When they sense
a big cat around,
    Impalas really cover ground.
They can leap thirty feet
    in a single bound.

Ants for breakfast,
     ants for lunch.
One at a time
     or all in a bunch.
Ants for soup,
     ants for pie......
Gotta have ants or die.

The gerenuk has a very long neck
that works for grazing high.
Beats the competition....
(till the giraffes come by).

A professor had the idea
that chimpanzees relate:
if they only had a voice box,
they would do more than mate.
　　Well, they got a chimp a tutor,
　　and a Macintosh computer...
Now he doesn't even date.

Meerkats live in
complex groups.
There are sentries,
hunters, teachers.
They are so well
organized
maybe there are
preachers?

Is the lizard smiling
'cause he's sly?
Or did this mellow
green and yellow fellow
catch a fly?

The giant tortoise looks old,
And old it may be.
Older than the other animals we know.
It may have hatched
on the Galapagos
two hundred years ago.

Llamas carry burdens without complaint,
  if they are loaded with restraint.
If one overloads these beasts...they'll try,
  then lose their cool, and spit right in your eye!

You can't insult an armadillo.
Call him ugly, call him yellow..
    Armi doesn't feel the sting,
    Armi doesn't feel a thing...
He is such a thick-skinned fellow.

What is this beast of central Asia?
Some kind of ox or goat?
The takin has us guessing.
Perhaps some antelope?

From Siberia to the Caspian Sea
the pallas cat lives wild and free.
Very fiesty, very shrewd....
a tiny cat with attitude.

Three weeks of beauty
   after three years in cocoon.
The adult moth is dying,
   dying oh so soon.

If you ever come back as a monkey,
a langur's a good one to be.
Most Hindus consider them sacred....
Good karma, good destiny.

Index of Animals

Roger C. Birkel is Director of The Baltimore Zoo. His conservation work with wildlife has taken him around the world where he has photographed animals both in the wild and in zoos.

Philip Macht is the author of WONDERPUP, GREAT MOUNTAIN, CIRCLES IN THE SAND, DANNYBIRD, the play BIGMAK, the verse for PUMPKIN ART, and the book and lyrics for the musical CIRCLES IN THE SAND in collaboration with his son, the composer Robert Macht.

TO THE ZOO

The TV nature shows are great,
---all that hunting, all that mating---
....educating....fascinating.
Still, the pictures can't compare
  with the joy of being there.
So take me out to the nearest zoo.
 There's nothing I would rather do
    than hear the local lions roar,
    or watch the seals perform for more.
I want to see what I can see,
    and I want the animals to look at me.